295

D1483703

How to Make and dress a doll

How to
Make and dress a doll

Gillian Lockwood
photographs by Geoffrey Drury

Studio Vista

Studio Vista a division of
Cassell & Collier Macmillan Publishers Limited
35 Red Lion Square, London WCIR 4SG
Sydney, Auckland, Toronto, Johannesburg

An affiliate of the Macmillan Publishing Co. Inc.
New York

Filmset and printed by BAS Printers Limited, Wallop, Hampshire

ISBN 0 289 70551 7

Contents

How to use this book

First make your doll, then you can follow the book through from front to back, or use the index to find the clothes you would most like to make.

Most of the things in the book will look better if pressed with an iron. Get your mother to help or to show you how to use an iron and which heat setting is right. Then you will not burn yourself or your handiwork.

Pins, needles and scissors are very sharp. Please be careful when you use them, and do not leave them lying around to hurt someone else.

preparing a pattern

Take a sheet of greaseproof paper, place it over the drawing in the book and trace the outline. Write its number on it with any other details you need.

Cut along the traced line and you have your pattern. This will give you a doll, or clothes for a doll, 27 cm high.

The broken line on the pattern means that the edge of the paper must be placed against a fold on the material. The dotted line shows where you can cut the pattern away to make a different garment. The fine dashed line is the seam line.

▬▬▬ ▬▬▬ ▬▬▬ ▬▬▬ ▬▬ broken line

• • • • • • • • • • • • • • • • • • • dotted line

— — — — — — — — — fine dashed line

making up the patterns

You can sew the doll's garments using a sewing machine or running stitch, or you can glue them using a fabric glue such as Copydex. The clothes can be washed if you use Copydex. Drawings in the book show you both ways of making up the garments. Follow whichever you prefer.

How to make the doll

You need:
flesh coloured material (cotton, winceyette or jersey);
matching cotton thread; pins; scissors; cut up stockings,
kapok or foam pieces for stuffing; wool in a natural
colour (25 gm or 1 oz ball); a thick needle; glue; felt the
colour of eyes; a one penny piece; soft pencil, needle
and pink embroidery thread

Trace and cut out this pattern.

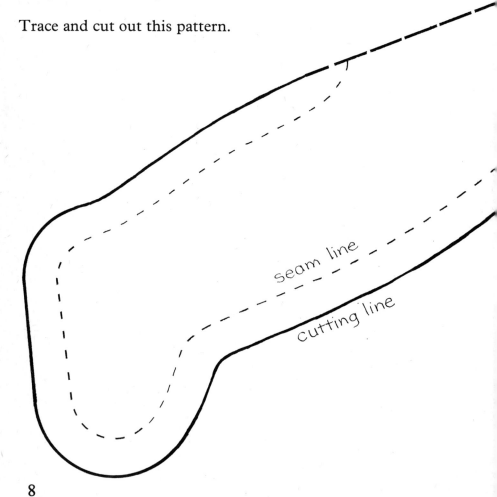

seam line

cutting line

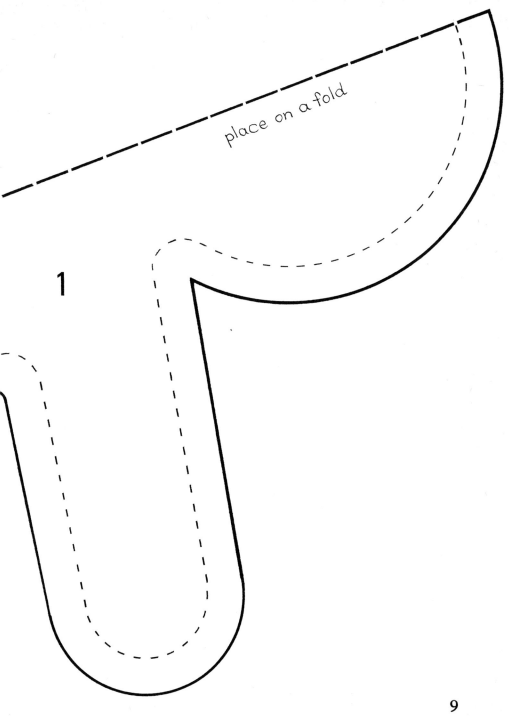

place on a fold

1

9

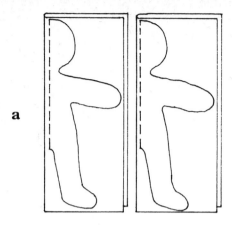

a

Fold the material and pin the pattern to it. Make sure the edge marked 'fold' is on the fold of the material, **a**. Cut round the edge of the pattern. Use the same pattern to cut another piece of material for the other side of the doll.

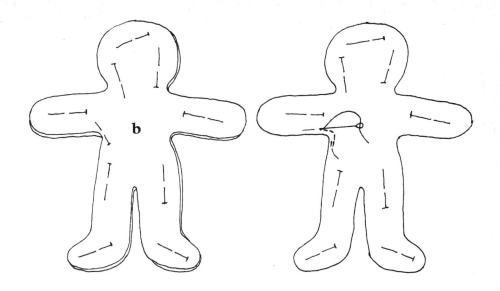

Pin the right sides of the material together **b**. Sew along the seam line using running stitch. Leave an opening under one arm and fasten off the thread firmly, **c**. If you can use a sewing machine for this, it will make the seam stronger.

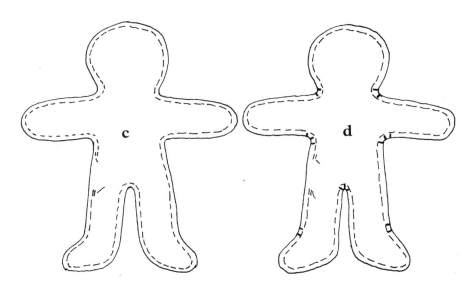

Carefully, make a small cut with the scissors in the curves, **d** (page 11). Turn the doll right side out and stuff it. Use a small amount of stuffing at a time working it into the feet, legs, arms and head before you start on the body. Oversew the underarm opening and fasten off the thread firmly, **e**.

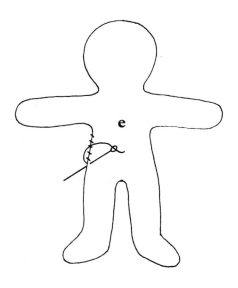

Hair

short hair
Wind half a 25 gm ball of wool round the narrow width of this book. Slip the wool off the book and tie it tightly at the centre.

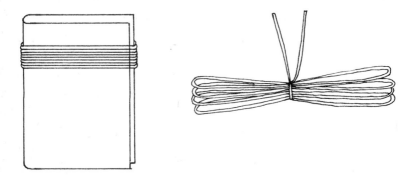

Cut through the loops and fan out the wool into a circle. Spread glue on the centre of the circle and on the top, sides and back of the head.

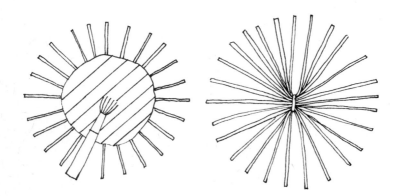

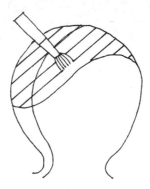

Press the hair firmly onto the head and trim it to a fringe and bob or a smooth curve.

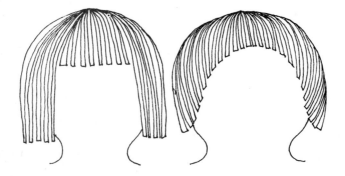

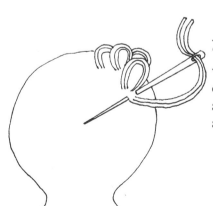

short curls
Thread a thick needle
with a double thickness
of wool and, working in
all directions, make loops
all over the head.

plaits

Wind three-quarters of a 25 gm ball of wool round this book from top to bottom. Cut through the loops at one end.

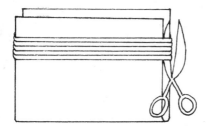

Tie a knot in the centre of the length. Make two more knots on either side of the centre knot.

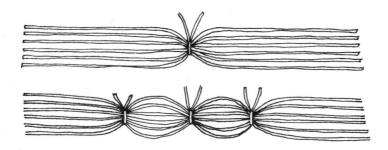

Spread some glue on the upper side of the centre portions of the wool.

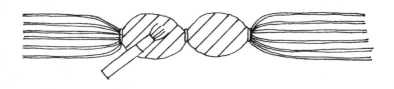

Press the hair onto the head and plait the ends.

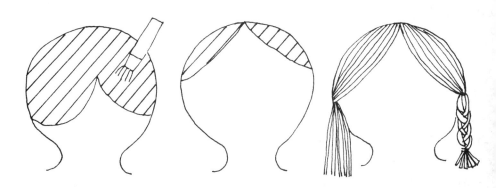

bunches

Wind half a 25 gm ball of wool round this book from top to bottom. Slip the wool off the book and tie a knot in the centre. Make two more knots on either side of the centre knot.

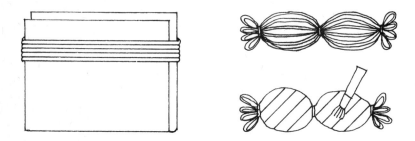

Spread glue on the upper side of the centre portions of the wool and on the head. Press the hair onto the doll's head.

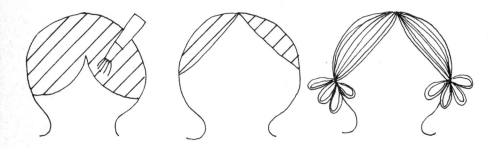

Adding the face

To make the eyes, lay the one penny piece on the felt
and draw round it twice, using a soft pencil. Cut out
the eyes and glue them onto the face.

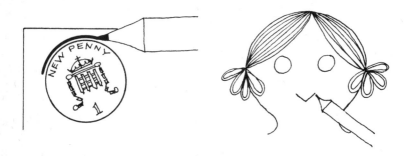

Mark a small 'v' on the face where the mouth will go.
Thread a long needle with pink embroidery thread and
tie a knot in the end. Bring the needle through from the
back of the head (the knot will be hidden by the hair)
and make the mouth as shown in the drawings. Take the
needle through to the back of the head on the last
stitch and fasten off the thread.

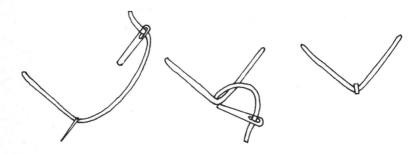

Good Morning

Vest and knickers

You need:
an old vest or similar fine knitted material
glue or matching thread
15 cm (or 6 in) length of narrow elastic

vest
Trace and cut out pattern No. 2 (page 24). Fold the
material, **a**, and pin the pattern onto it. Cut out the
pieces and glue, **b** or sew, **c**, the side seams. Turn the
vest inside out, so that the seams are on the inside.

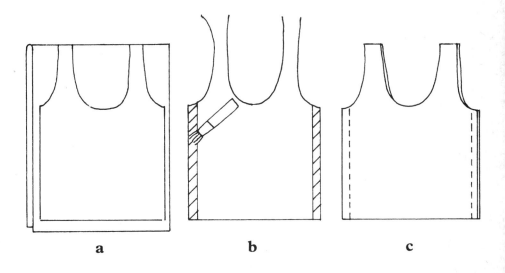

a   b   c

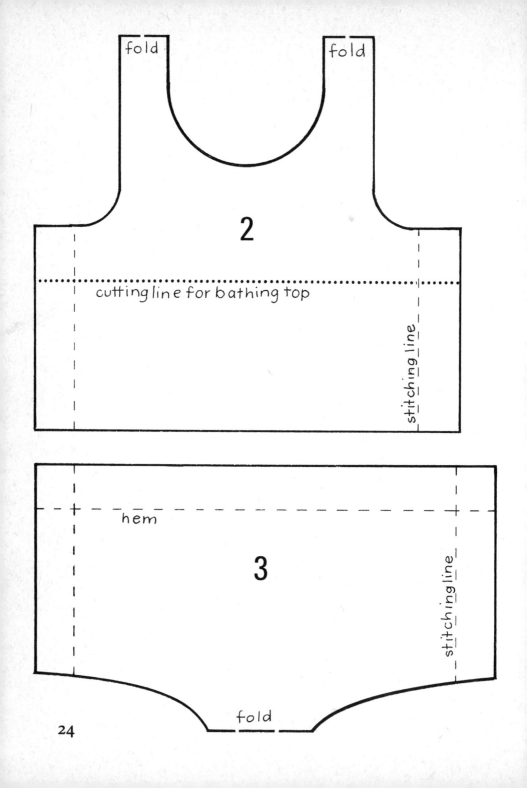

fold   fold

2

cutting line for bathing top

stitching line

3

hem

stitching line

fold

24

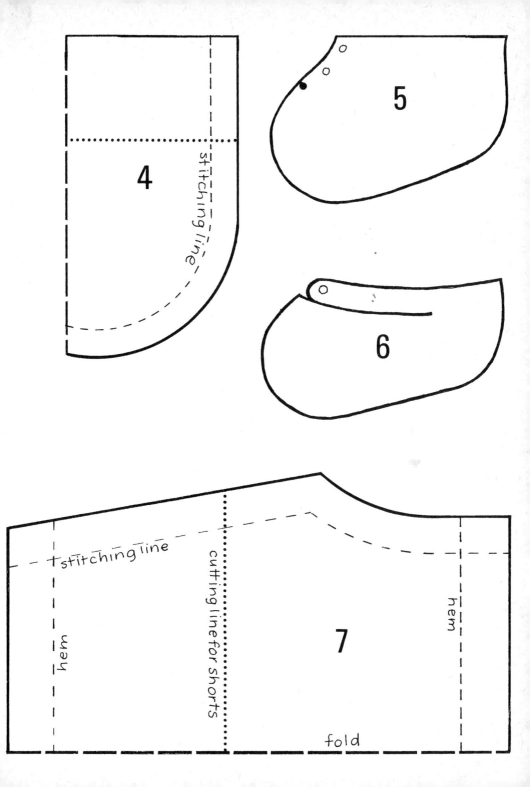

4

stitching line

5

6

stitching line

hem

cutting line for shorts

7

hem

fold

knickers

Trace and cut out pattern No. 3 (page 24). Fold the material, **a**, and pin on the pattern. Cut it out. Sew or glue the side seam, **b** or **c**.

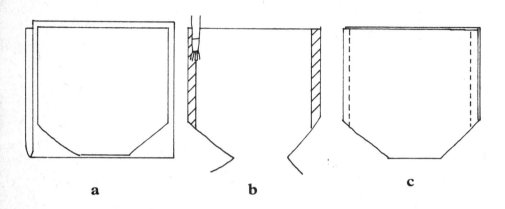

a   b   c

Join the elastic into a circle, overlapping the ends, and stitch them firmly together. Pull the top of the knickers through the elastic, **d**, and glue or sew a narrow hem over it, **e** or **f**. Turn the knickers inside out, so that the seams are on the inside.

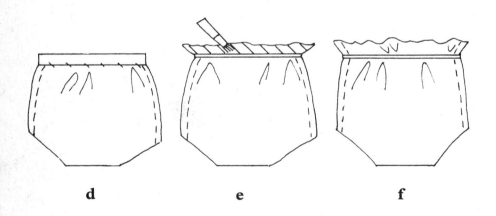

d   e   f

Shoes

You need:
felt or thin leather
matching thread
string, narrow tape or ribbon
scissors and a knitting needle

Trace and cut out pattern No. 5 (boots) or 6 (shoes) (page 25). Using a soft pencil draw around the pattern onto the felt four times. Cut the pieces out carefully. Oversew the shoes together in pairs, leaving the boy's boots open at the front to take laces. Make holes with the point of a knitting needle where the laces are to be and thread them with string, tape or ribbon.

Socks

You need:
fine knitted material (old vest)
glue or matching thread

Trace and cut out pattern No. 4 (page 25) for long or
short socks. Fold the material and place the pattern in
position. Make sure that the dotted fold line on the
pattern is against the fold of the material. Cut round
the pattern. Repeat this for the second sock. Make two
5 mm seams on the curved edges using glue or running
stitch.

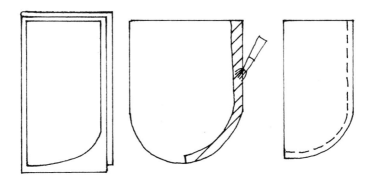

Time for play

Tee shirt

You need:
stretchy non-fray material
needle and cotton or glue
scissors

Trace and cut out pattern
No. 8 (page 31) with short
sleeves. Fold the material in
half and pin the pattern to
it, making sure the fold
line is against the fold of
the material.

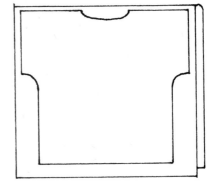

Cut it out. Cut down the centre front to the position
of the large dot marked on the pattern. Sew or glue
the underarm seams. Paste the glue on the right side of
the material, or sew the right sides together. Turn
the tee shirt the right way out so that the seams are
on the inside.

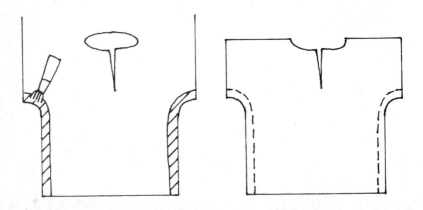

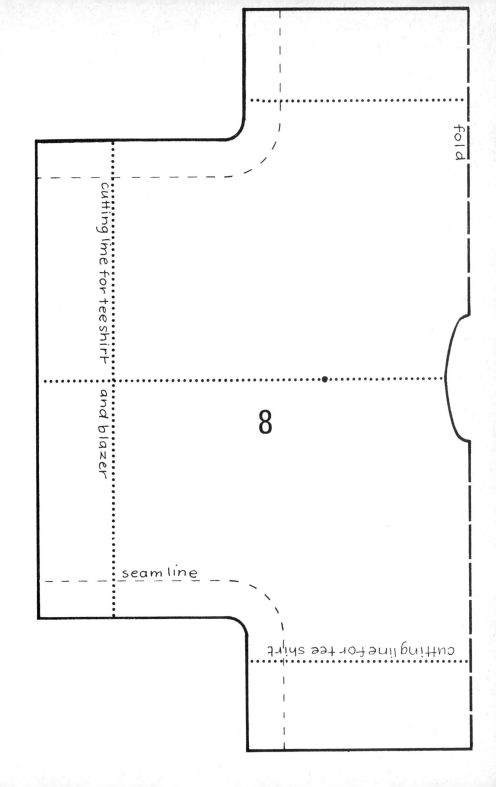

fold

cutting line for tee shirt

and blazer

seam line

8

cutting line for tee shirt

Trousers

You need:
denim, thin wool or jersey material
glue or matching thread
15 cm (or 6 in) length of elastic
scissors

Trace and cut out pattern No. 7 (page 25). Choose long or short legs. Fold the material and pin the pattern to it. Cut it out. Do the same for the other leg. Sew or glue the seams down the front and back of the trousers. Spread the glue carefully on the right side of the material or, using running stitch, sew the right sides together.

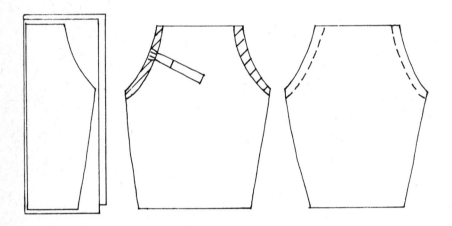

Opposite
Time for play. The girl's cotton dress (page 37) is trimmed with bias binding and braid. The boy's denim trousers (page 32) and tee shirt (page 30) are just right for the garden

Make a seam down each leg in the same way.

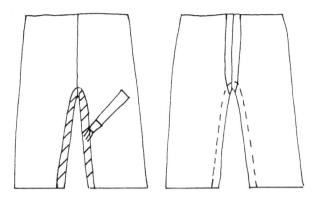

Finish the top with elastic as for the knickers on page 26. If you are using denim, fray the bottom of the legs. With other materials turn under a small hem, and glue or sew it neatly.

Opposite
Time for a walk. Both the boy's blazer and beret (pages 40 and 60) and the girl's cap and coat (pages 61 and 41) are easy to make

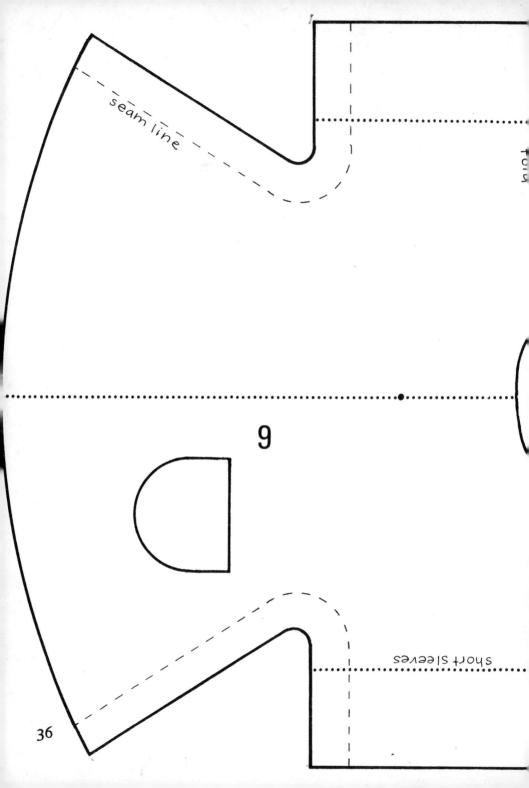

seam line

fold

9

36

short sleeves

Dress

You need:
any thin material
glue or matching thread
scissors

Trace and cut out pattern
No. 6 (page 36) with short
or long sleeves. Fold the
material and pin it to the
pattern. Cut it out, not
forgetting the curve for the
neck. Cut down the centre
front as far as the large dot
marked on the pattern.

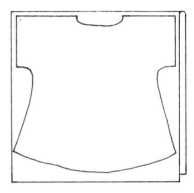

Make two seams under the arms using glue or running
stitch. Spread the glue on the right side of the material
or sew with running stitch with the right sides of the
material together. Turn the dress the right way out. The
seams will be on the inside.

If the material does not fray, you can leave the edges.
Or you can finish them in any of the ways suggested on
page 38.

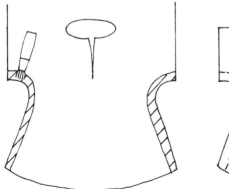

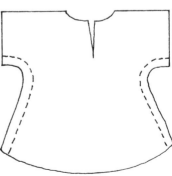

Trimmings

bias binding
Place the right side of the opening binding to the right side of the edge of the material to be bound, **a**. Sew together using running stitch. Take the binding over to the wrong side and hem down neatly, **b**.

Binding can also be stitched or glued onto the front of the material as stripes.

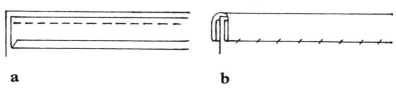

a   **b**

lace
Lace can be added in two ways:
1 Turn up a narrow hem, on the wrong side of the material, along the edge to be trimmed, **c**. Place the lace over the hem and using small stitches, sew through both lace and hem, **d**.

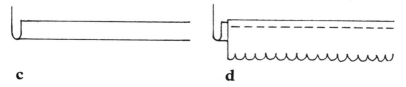

c   **d**

2 If the material is non-fray the lace can be added directly to the edge. With the right side of the material and the lace together, use small oversewing stitches to join them, **e**.

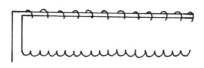

e

38

ric-rac braid

Ric-rac makes a nice scalloped edge. Turn up a narrow hem on the wrong side of the material along the edge to be trimmed, **f**. Glue or stitch the ric-rac in position, **g**.

Ric-rac can be glued or stitched onto the front of the material as stripes.

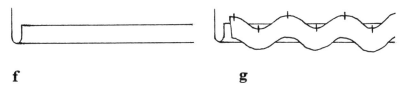

f   **g**

ribbon rose

Take a short length of narrow ribbon. Work a row of running stitches very close to one edge, **h**. Pull up the thread to form gathers, **i**. Roll up the gathered ribbon into a rose, **j**, and sew the roll at the back to hold it together, **k**.

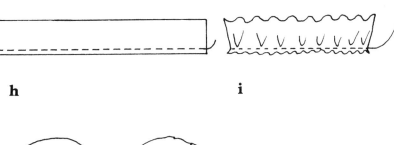

h   **i**

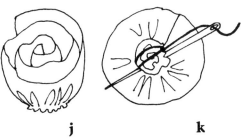

j   **k**

blanket stitch

Use thick thread or wool. Start the first stitch with running stitch, **1**, then continue along the edge, **m**. To turn a corner, do the same type of stitch but put the needle through the same hole for the last stitch of the old side, the corner stitch and the first stitch on the new side, **n**.

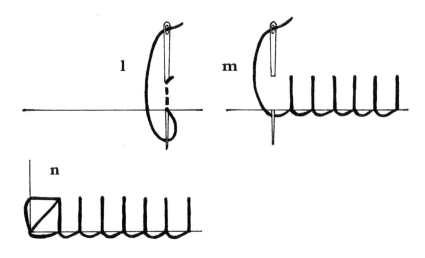

Blazer

You need:
felt, woollen or non-fray material
glue or matching thread
bias binding or narrow ribbon
scissors

Trace and cut out pattern No. 8 (page 31). Then follow the instructions for the coat, page 41. You can trim the blazer with ribbon, binding or blanket stitch (page 38).

Coat

You need:
a piece of felt 30 × 21 cm (or 12 × 16½ in)
glue or matching thread
scissors

Trace and cut out pattern No. 9 (page 36), with pockets if you want them. Fold the felt and pin the pattern in position. Cut it out, not forgetting the curve for the neck. Cut down the centre front to the bottom edge. Cut out the pockets from scraps left over. Glue the seams or sew them with running stitch. Turn the coat the right way out and glue or hem the pockets in position.

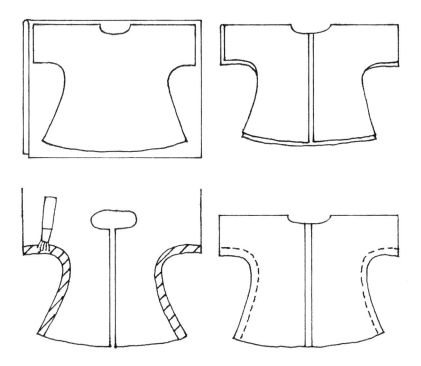

On the beach

Bathing trunks and top

You need:
stretchy non-fray material
glue or matching thread
15 cm (or 6 in) length of elastic

Cut out and make up exactly as the vest and knickers on page 23.

Beach wrap

You need:
one attractive face flannel or towelling material
glue or matching thread
30 cm (or 12 in) of cotton cord or tape
scissors

Trace and cut out pattern No. 8 (page 31), using the longer length. Cut it out and make it up in the same way as the coat (page 41). Work round the edges with blanket stitch (page 40).

Skirt

You need:
a piece of felt 28 × 15 cm (or 11 × 6 in)
glue or matching thread
1 press stud
braid for trimming

Trace and cut out pattern No. 10 (page 46). Pin the pattern to the felt and cut it out. If you have pinking shears, use them to give a fancy edge. Fold the felt in half and make a seam using glue or running stitch. Leave an opening at the waist and with the skirt the right way out, sew on a small press stud. Sew or glue on some braid or felt shapes as a trimming.

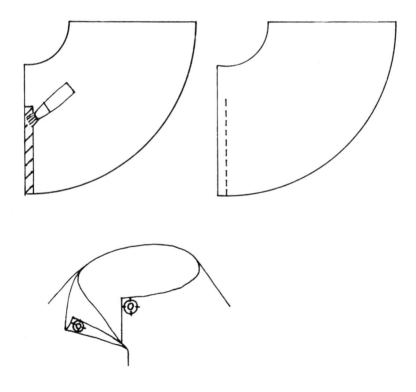

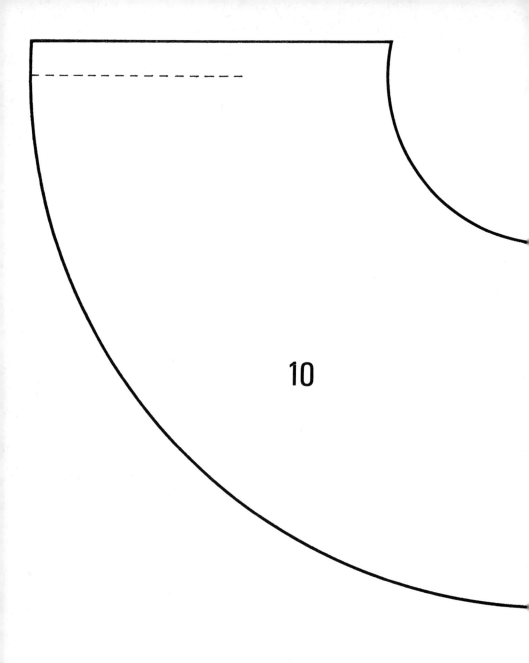

10

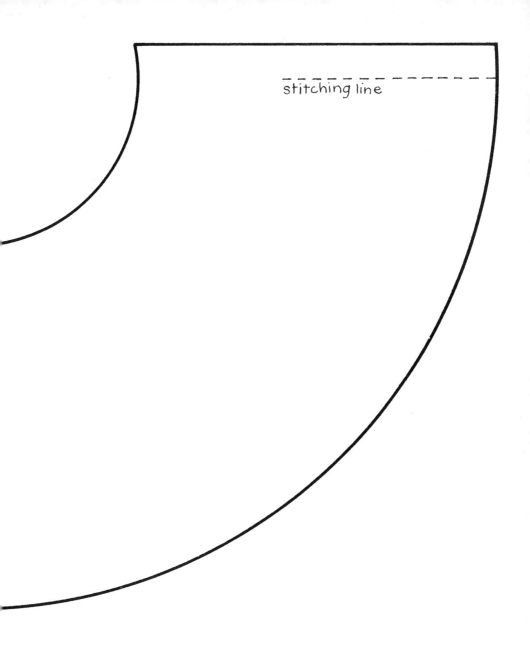

stitching line

Poncho

You need:
a piece of woollen material 20 cm (or 8 in) square
wool or thick thread

Fray all four sides 1 cm (about $\frac{3}{8}$ in). Cut a diagonal opening 8 cm (or $3\frac{1}{4}$ in) long across the centre of the square.

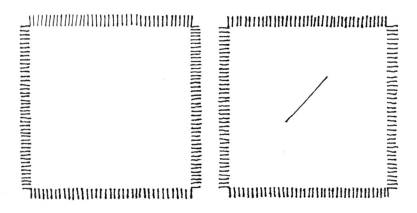

Work blanket stitch round the opening, page 40.

Party time

Party dress

You need:
any exciting material
90 cm (or 1 yard) of ribbon
glue or matching thread
scissors

Trace and cut out pattern No. 11 (page 56). Fold the material and pin the pattern in position. Cut it out, not forgetting the curve for the neck. Sew or glue the seams. Spread the glue on the right side of the material, or sew in running stitch with the right sides together. Turn the dress the right way out.

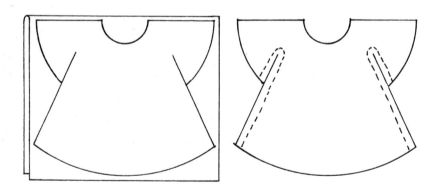

If the material is non-fray you can leave the edges, or you can finish them with a narrow hem or lace (page 38). Make one or two roses (page 39) and sew them with ribbon to the front of the dress.

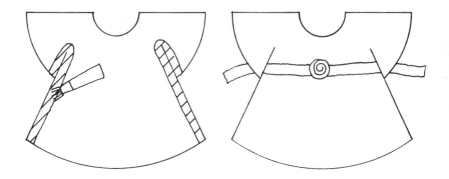

Opposite
These two are just off to bed, the girl wearing a pretty nightdress (page 54) and the boy his patterned pyjamas (page 59).

Time for bed

Nightdress

You need:
thin non-fray material
glue or matching thread
1·15 m (or 1¼ yds) of narrow lace

Trace and cut out pattern No. 11 (page 56), with no sleeves. Fold the material and pin the pattern to it. Cut it out. Sew or glue the two underarm seams, spreading the glue carefully on the right side of the material, or sew the right sides together using running stitch. Trim all the edges with narrow lace (page 38).

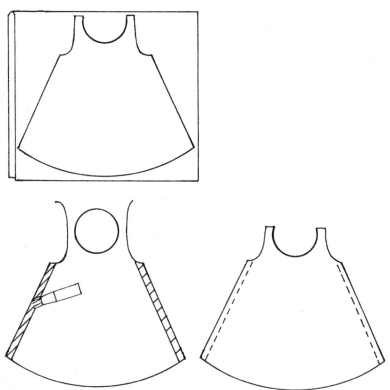

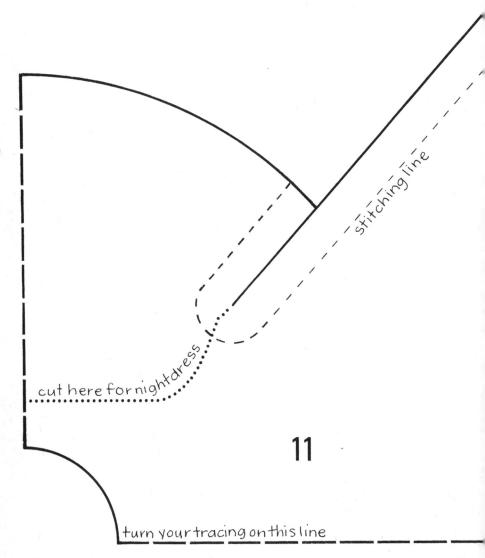

stitching line

cut here for nightdress

11

turn your tracing on this line

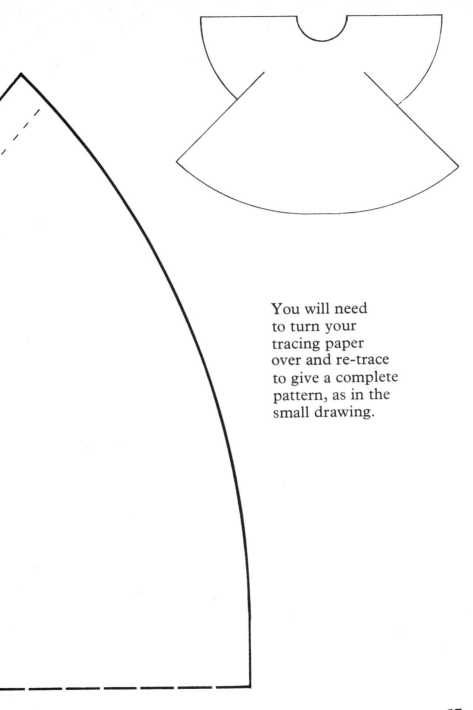

You will need
to turn your
tracing paper
over and re-trace
to give a complete
pattern, as in the
small drawing.

Dressing gown

You need:
thin non-fray material
glue or matching thread
1·60 m (or 1¾ yds) of narrow lace
45 cm (or ½ yard) of narrow ribbon

Trace and cut out pattern No. 11 (page 56) with sleeves.
Fold the material and pin the pattern to it. Cut it out.
Cut down the centre front to the bottom edge and glue
or sew the two underarm seams. Turn the dressing
gown the right side out.

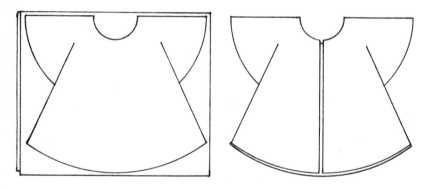

Trim all the edges with narrow lace, (page 38). Cut the
narrow ribbon in half and sew it to either side of the
neck to make ties.

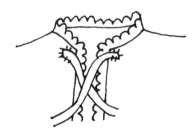

Pyjamas

You need:
thin non-fray material or thin cotton
glue or matching thread
15 cm (or 6 in) narrow elastic
two small buttons
two small press studs

Using patterns No. 7 (page 25) and No. 8 (page 31) make up the pyjamas following the directions for trousers (page 32) and blazer (page 40). If the material is non-fray you can leave the edges. If it is cotton, finish them with a narrow hem or bound edges (page 38).

Finish the jacket with two buttons sewn over the press studs for fastening.

Bits and pieces

Beret

You need:
soft woollen or other material
small quantity of wool
short length of binding

Cut out a 20 cm (or 8 in) circle from the material (a dessert plate is about this size). Using double thread, stitch close to the edge around the circle in running stitch. Draw up the thread until the circle measures 7 cm (or 2¾ in) across. Cover the raw edges with binding.

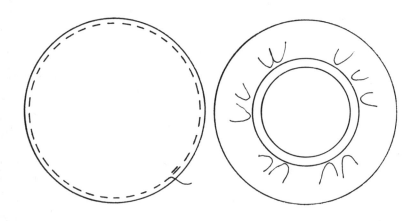

Wind some wool around three fingers, slip it off. Knot the centre of the bundle tightly. Cut the loops on each side of the knot and stitch the pom pom to the centre of the beret.

Cap

You need:
scraps of felt
sewing cotton

Trace pattern No. 14 (page 63). Pin the pattern onto felt and cut it out. Repeat this five times, so that you have six sections. Join the sections together with oversewing to form a skull cap.

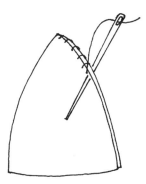

If the cap is for a boy add a peak, pattern No. 15, oversewing it into position. Add a tassel to the top of the girl's cap.

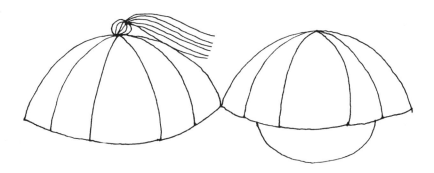

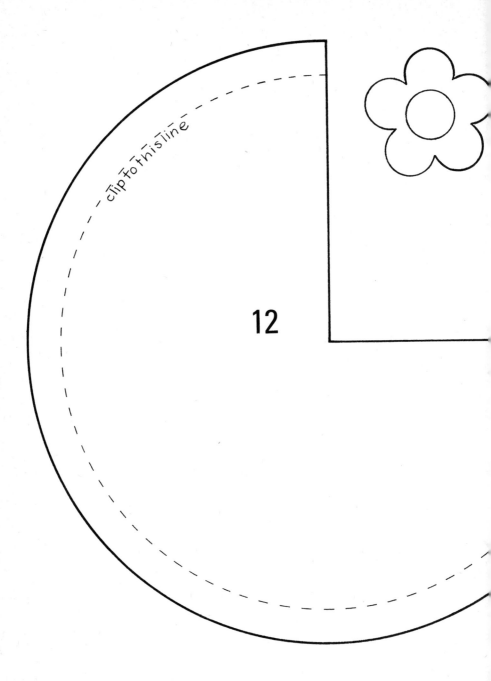

clip to this line

12

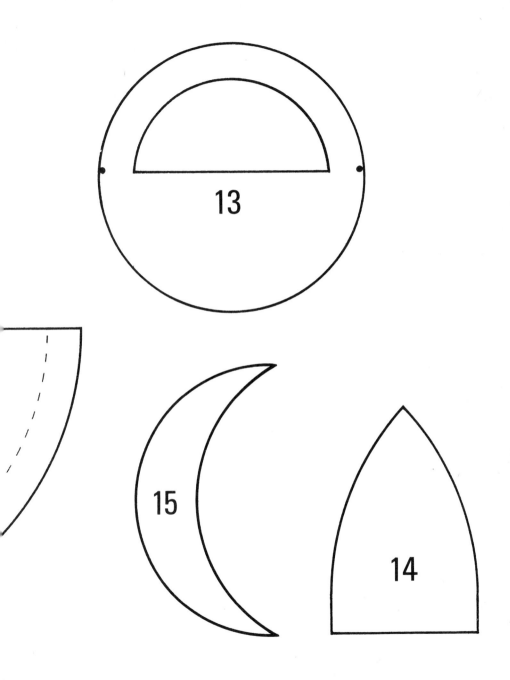

13

15

14

Sun hat

You need:
felt for hat and flowers
glue

Trace pattern No. 12 (page 62). Pin the pattern to the felt and cut it out. Also cut out some flowers. Make 1 cm (or ⅜ in) snips all around the brim close together, with scissors.

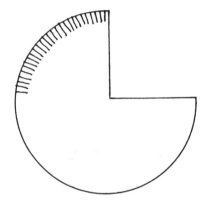

Spread glue on one side at the back of the hat. Press the other side onto the glued edge, overlapping the two.

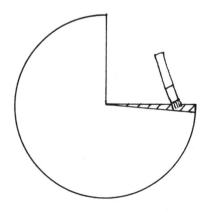

Sun bonnet and apron

You need
1 lace edged or pattern bordered hanky
80 cm (or 32 in) of narrow ribbon or tape cut into four

Cut the hanky into two equal halves. Make a 2 cm (or $\frac{3}{4}$ in) hem on the wrong side of both pieces along the cut edges. Using double thread sew the hem with running stitch.

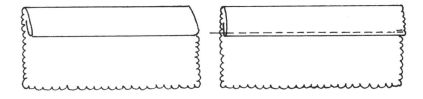

sun bonnet
Draw up the thread as tightly as you can and join the two ends together into a circle. Add ribbon to the two corners for ties.

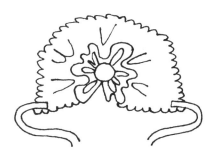

65

apron

For the apron draw up the thread until the gathered hem is 10 cm (or 4 in) wide. Fasten off the thread firmly. Join the ribbon on either side of the hem as ties.

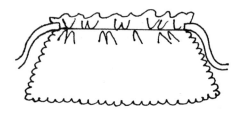

Bag

You need:
scraps of felt
thread

Trace pattern No. 13 (page 63). Pin the pattern onto the felt and cut it out. Repeat this for the other half. Join the two pieces together at the lower edge with oversewing.

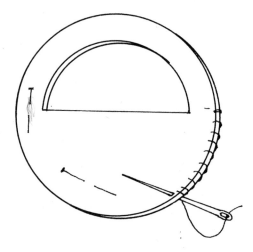

Index